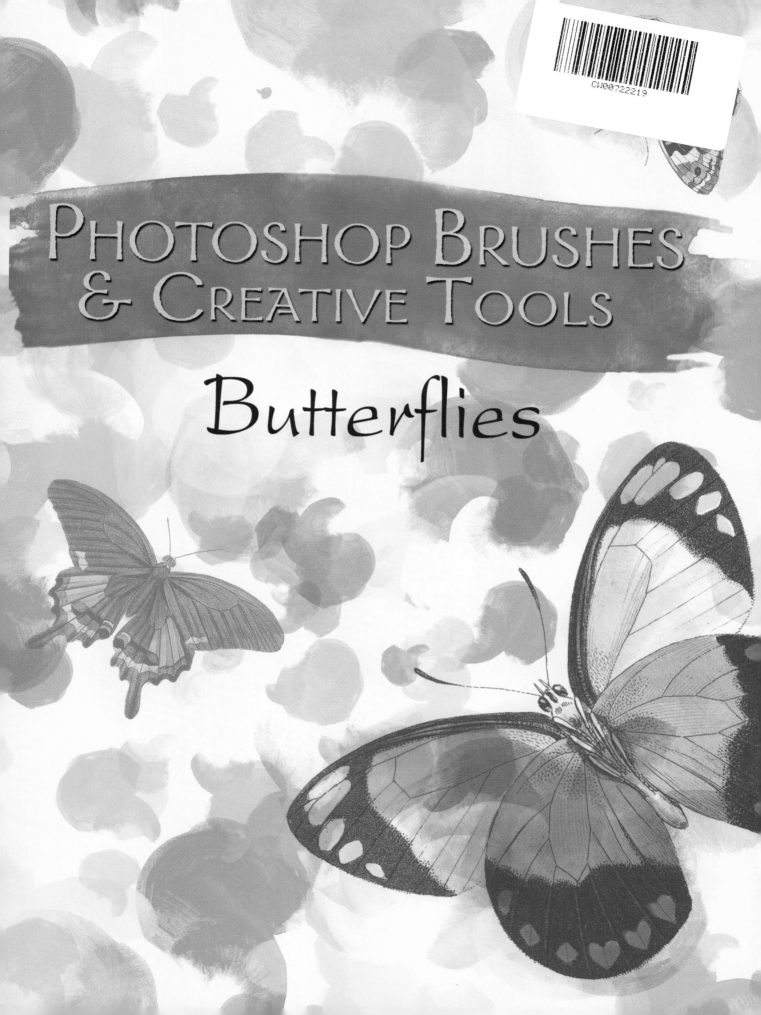

PHOTOSHOP BRUSHES
& CREATIVE TOOLS

Butterflies

Planet Friendly Publishing
✔ Made in the United States
✔ Printed on Recycled Paper
  Text: 10%   Cover: 10%
Learn more: www.greenedition.org

GREEN EDITION

At Dover Publications we're committed to producing books in an earth-friendly manner and to helping our customers make greener choices.

Manufacturing books in the United States ensures compliance with strict environmental laws and eliminates the need for international freight shipping, a major contributor to global air pollution.

And printing on recycled paper helps minimize our consumption of trees, water and fossil fuels. The text of *Photoshop Brushes and Creative Tools CD-ROM and Book: Butterflies* was printed on paper made with 10% post-consumer waste, and the cover was printed on paper made with 10% post-consumer waste. According to Environmental Defense's Paper Calculator, by using this innovative paper instead of conventional papers, we achieved the following environmental benefits:

Trees Saved: 5 • Air Emissions Eliminated: 387 pounds
Water Saved: 1,574 gallons • Solid Waste Eliminated: 206 pounds

For more information on our environmental practices, please visit us online at www.doverpublications.com/green

Bibliographical Note

Photoshop Brushes and Creative Tools CD-ROM and Book: Butterflies, is a new work, first published by Dover Publications, Inc., in 2009.

Dover Electronic Clip Art®

International Standard Book Number
ISBN-13: 978-0-486-99058-3
ISBN-10: 0-486-99058-3

For technical support, contact:
Telephone: 1 (617) 249-0245
Fax: 1 (617) 249-0245
Email: dover@artimaging.com
Internet: **http://www.dovertechsupport.com**
The fastest way to receive technical support is via email or the Internet.

Manufactured in the United States by Courier Corporation
99058301
www.doverpublications.com

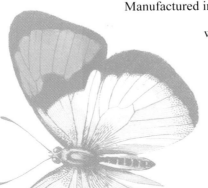

What's on the CD?

Included on the CD is a collection of 123 Butterfly Brushes and 40 Butterfly Custom Shapes, for use with Adobe Photoshop (versions CS–CS4) and Photoshop Elements. The images for these brushes and shapes have been carefully selected from the Dover archive of rare, old sourcebooks, and are crafted to give you the finest image quality and greatest utility.

We've also included a set of 21 special Texture Brushes to quickly create subtle, painterly backgrounds, and a set of 20 Photoshop Styles, which dramatically expand the expressive range of the brushes and shapes.

Also on the CD-ROM is Dover Design Manager, a simple graphics editing program for Windows that will allow you to view grayscale images of the brushes, shapes, and styles included on the CD-ROM.

Brushes

Dover Photoshop Brushes make a dazzling array of marks with any tool that utilizes the Brushes Palette in Photoshop– Paintbrushes, Pencil, Erasers, and Stamp Tools. They can be used to quickly create photographic and painterly effects, or employed graphically as digital 'rubber stamps'. With experimentation, more complex creative effects can be mastered to execute sophisticated shape and color dynamics, and pattern-scattering. The brushes are easy to install, and quick to master.

Custom Shapes

Custom Shapes provide a quick method for placing editable, vector shapes into Photoshop compositions. After installation, simply choose one of the Dover Butterfly Shapes from the Shapes pull-down menu. The vector outline that appears in your composition can be edited using the Pen and Path Selection Tools, and colored and styled using pre-set Photoshop Styles or simple color fills. Because Custom Shapes are vector graphics, and therefore not adversely effected by extreme enlargement, they are particularly well-suited for large-scale graphic arts projects

Styles

Photoshop Styles are pre-set combinations of effects that can dramatically change the appearance of custom shapes, brushes, images, text and vector objects. Typical effects are shadow, glow, bevel and color overlay. Our styles are meant to complement and enliven the the shapes and brushes on the CD; they can be used 'as is' with a simple click of a button, or customized to create a limitless set of variations.

What's in the Book?

The Gallery section has color illustrations that depict some of the visual effects that can be created using the tools and techniques in this publication; all were created with the brushes, shapes and styles that are included on the CD ROM. The Tutorials section contains easy, step-by-step instructions for installing each of the tools into your version of Photoshop, and descriptions and usage instructions for the wide variety of creative controls that effect the ways in which these brushes 'paint' digitally. The Index section of this book contains numbered illustrations, for quick reference, of each brush, shape and style available on the CD.

Gallery

050

095

111

S 018

BRS 011

ST 015

Shape Dynamics,
Scattering, Spacing,
Color Dynamics,
Opacity, Layers Styles

5

Gallery

021

024

035

S 026

BRS 004

ST 009

Shape Dynamics,
Scattering, Spacing,
Color Dynamics, Texture
Opacity, Layers Styles

Gallery

047

061

092

S 009

BRS 018

ST 001

Shape Dynamics,
Scattering, Spacing,
Color Dynamics,
Opacity, Layers Styles

9

038

043

123

S 031

BRS 009

ST 008

Shape Dynamics,
Scattering, Spacing,
Color Dynamics,
Opacity, Layers Styles

Gallery

032

073

103

S 024

BRS 020

ST 013

Spacing, Color Dynamics,
Opacity, Layers Styles

13

Brushes Palette Overview

Photoshop Elements Users:

Please see the PhotoshopElements.PDF file
on the accompanying CD for special instructions.

The Brush Palette

With the Brushes Palette, you can choose preset
brushes, similar to the Brush Preset Picker, or
you can modify brush tip options to change
how the paint is applied to the canvas.

At the bottom of the palette is the brush
stroke preview that allows you to view what
the current brush stroke will look like.

1. Lock and Unlock will save the variations
   applied to the Brush Tip.

2. Brush Selection

3. Brush Settings and Controls.

4. Brush Stroke Preview Window.

5. Brush Tip Diameter Control.

6. Brush Tip Angle Controls.

7. The Spacing Control will vary the
   distance between each brush mark
   during the stroke.

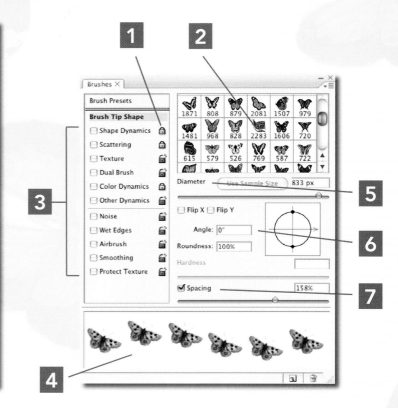

Changing the Brush Presets View

1. Click the arrow in the upper right
   corner of the Brushes palette.

2. Choose either Text Only, Small
   Thumbnail, Large Thumbnail,
   Small List, Large List or Stroke
   Thumbnail to change how
   the brush presets are displayed.

How to Load Brushes

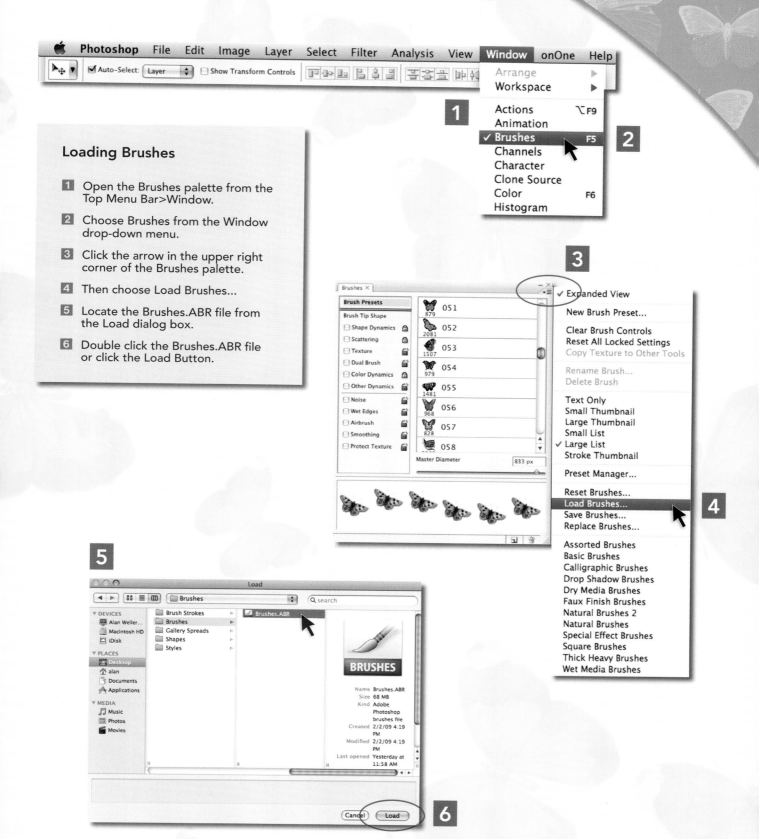

Loading Brushes

1. Open the Brushes palette from the Top Menu Bar>Window.

2. Choose Brushes from the Window drop-down menu.

3. Click the arrow in the upper right corner of the Brushes palette.

4. Then choose Load Brushes...

5. Locate the Brushes.ABR file from the Load dialog box.

6. Double click the Brushes.ABR file or click the Load Button.

15

Shape Dynamics

Adding Shape Dynamics

Shape Dynamics will vary the brush marks during the stroke.

1 Size Jitter and Control will vary the size of the brush tips during the stroke.

2 Minimum Diameter controls the minimum brush size when Size Jitter or Size Control have been enabled.

3 Tilt scale will control the height of the brush before rotation when Size Control is set to Pen Tilt.

4 Angle Jitter and Control will vary the angle of the brush mark during the stroke.

5 The Roundness Jitter and Control will vary the roundness of the brush mark during the stroke.

6 Minimum Roundness sets the minimum roundness of the brush when Roundness Jitter or Roundness Control have been applied.

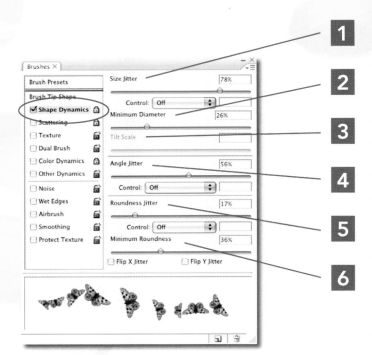

Scatter the Brush

Brush scattering will vary the percentage of marks in each brush stroke.

1 The Scatter and Control options will determine how the brush marks are dispersed throughout the brush stroke.

Marks are dispersed on a perpendicular axis to the stroke path when Both Axes is deselected.

2 Count will change the percentage of marks at each spacing interval.

Note: If the count is too high for the stroke being used, the effect may look distorted.

3 Count Jitter and Control will vary the Count Setting per each brush stroke.

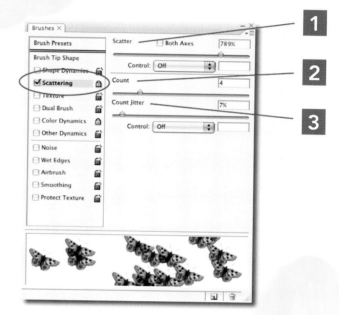

Texture

Brush Texture

The textured brush uses patterns to simulate painted strokes on a textured canvas.

1 Click the pattern sample square, and select a pattern from the pop-up palette.

Vary the pattern with the following options:

2 Scale will vary the size of the pattern inside the brush shape.

3 Texture Each Tip will apply the pattern to each individual brush tip rather than the brush stroke as a whole. This option must be selected for Depth variance to be available.

The Mode option will change how the brush and the pattern are combined.

4 The Depth option will vary how deeply the paint will penetrate the texture.

5 Minimum Depth is available when Depth Control is set to Fade, Pen Pressure, Pen Tilt, or Stylus Wheel, and Texture Each Tip is selected.

6 Depth Jitter and Control will vary the depth when Texture Each Tip is selected.

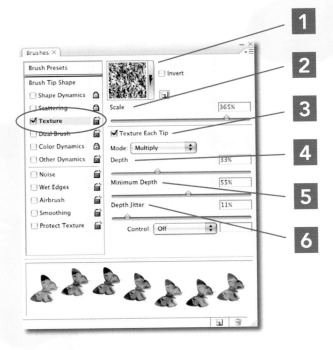

Color Dynamics

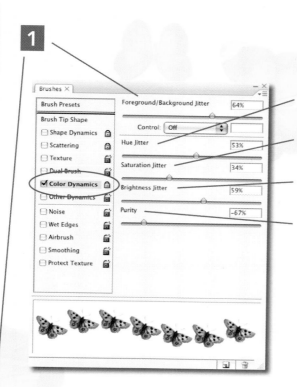

Color Dynamics

Color dynamics will vary the color of paint over the duration of the stroke.

1 The Foreground/Background Jitter will control how the paint varies between the foreground and background color in the tool bar.

2 Hue Jitter will change the percentage in which the hue can vary in the brush stroke.

3 Saturation Jitter will change the percentage in which the saturation can vary in the brush stroke.

4 The Brightness Jitter will vary the brightness of the paint during the brush stroke.

5 Purity will simply decrease or increase the saturation of the color.

Other Dynamics Brush Option

Other Dynamics

This option determines how the paint will change over the course of a stroke.

1 Opacity Jitter and Control will specify how the opacity of paint varies in a brush stroke.

Change the opacity by typing a number or use the slider control to enter a value of 1 to 100%.

To control the opacity variance of the brush stroke, select an option from the Control pop-up menu.

2 Flow Jitter and Control will specify how the flow of paint varies in a brush stroke.

Change the flow by typing a number or use the slider control to enter a value of 1 to 100%.

To control the flow variance of the brush stroke, select an option from the Control pop-up menu.

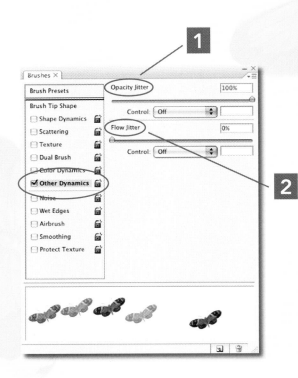

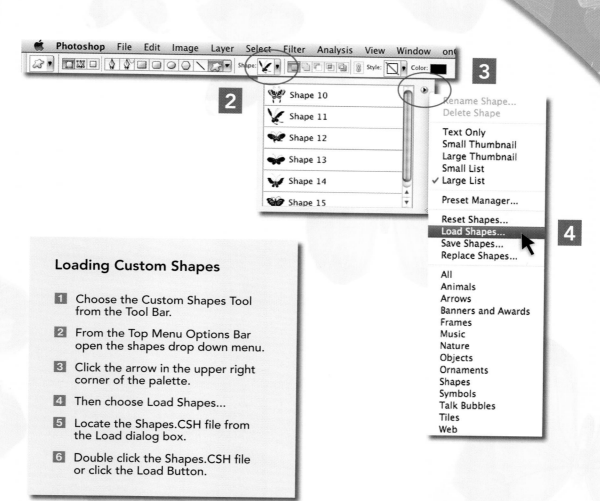

Loading Custom Shapes

1 Choose the Custom Shapes Tool from the Tool Bar.

2 From the Top Menu Options Bar open the shapes drop down menu.

3 Click the arrow in the upper right corner of the palette.

4 Then choose Load Shapes...

5 Locate the Shapes.CSH file from the Load dialog box.

6 Double click the Shapes.CSH file or click the Load Button.

Drawing Custom Shapes

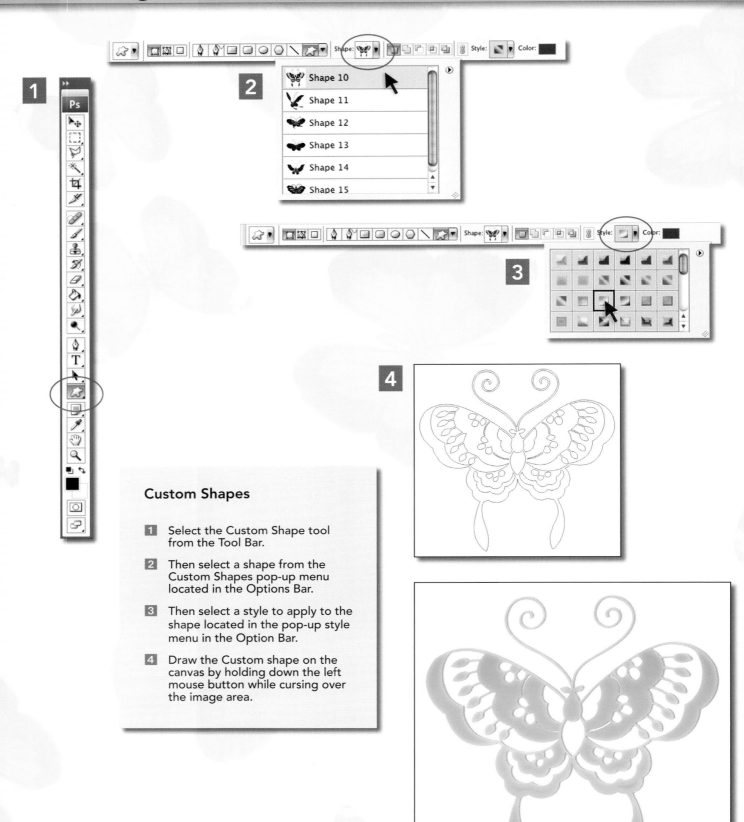

Custom Shapes

1. Select the Custom Shape tool from the Tool Bar.

2. Then select a shape from the Custom Shapes pop-up menu located in the Options Bar.

3. Then select a style to apply to the shape located in the pop-up style menu in the Option Bar.

4. Draw the Custom shape on the canvas by holding down the left mouse button while cursing over the image area.

Shape 10
Shape 11
Shape 12
Shape 13
Shape 14
Shape 15

Layer Styles Overview

Layer Styles

You can edit styles applied to a layer via the Layer Styles dialog box.

1 To open the Layer Styles dialog box double click the small FX symbol located to the right of the layer name.

2 In the Layer Styles dialog box the check boxes allow you to simply assign or unassign effect's without looking deeper into each individual effects options.

Click the name of the effect to view the options associated with it.

3 One or more of the following effects can be applied to create the layer style:

Drop Shadow, Inner Shadow, Outer Glow & Inner Glow, Bevel and Emboss, Satin, Color Overlay, Gradient Overlay, Pattern Overlay, and Stoke.

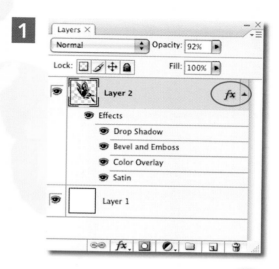

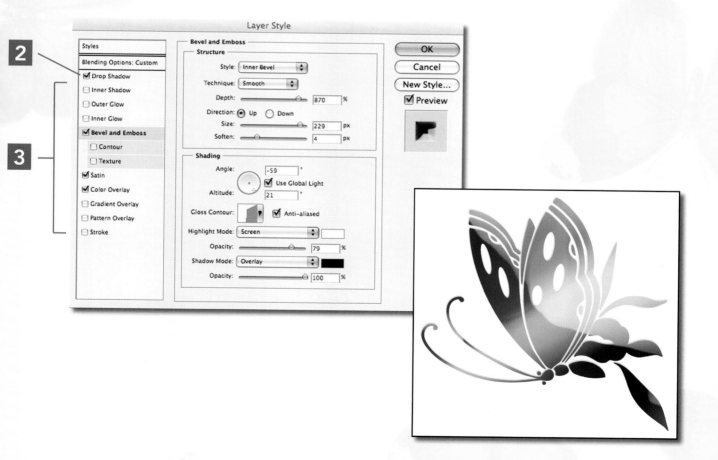

How to Load Styles

Loading Styles

1. Open the Styles palette from the Top Menu Bar>Window.

2. Choose Styles from the Window drop-down menu.

3. Click the arrow in the upper right corner of the Styles palette.

4. Then choose Load Styles...

5. Locate the Styles.ASL file from the Load dialog box.

6. Double click the Styles.ASL file or click the Load Button.

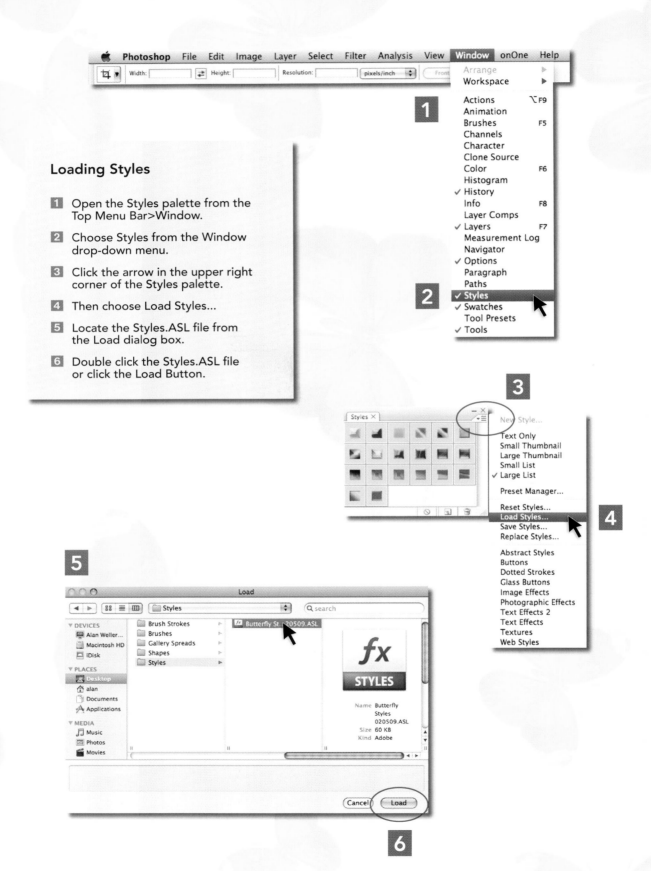

Styles Palette Overview

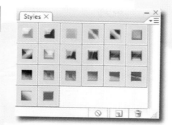

The Styles Palette

1. The Styles Palette lets you view and change layer styles by clicking on the desired thumbnail.

2. To change the view of the Styles Palette, Click the arrow in the upper right corner.

3. Select either Text Only, Small Thumbnail, Large Thumbnail, Small List or Large List from the pop-up menu.

4. To apply a style from the Styles Palette. Select the Image you are working on then simply click on the desired style.

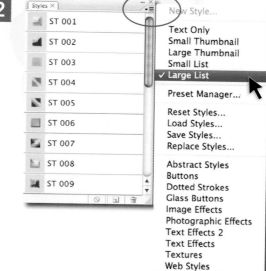

001

002

003

004

005

006

007

008

009

010

011

012

013

014

015

016

017

018

019

020

021

022

023

024

025

026

28

027

028

029

030

031

032

033

034

035

036

037

038

039

040

041

042

043

044

045

046

047

048

049

050

051

052

053

054

055

056

057

058

059

060

061

062

063

064

065

066

067

068

069

070

071

072

073

074

075

076

077

078

079

080

081

082

083

084

085

086

087

088

089

090

091

092

093

094

095

096

097

098

099

100

101

102

103

104

105

106

107

108

109

110

111

112

113

114

115

116

40

117

118

119

120

121

122

123

S 001

S 002

S 003

S 004

S 005

S 006

S 007

S 008

S 009

S 010

S 011

S 012

S 013

S 014

S 015

S 016

S 017

S 018

S 019

S 020

S 021

S 022

S 023

S 024

S 025

S 026

S 027

S 028

S 029

S 030

S 031

S 032

S 033

S 034

S 035

S 036

S 037

S 038

S 039

S 040

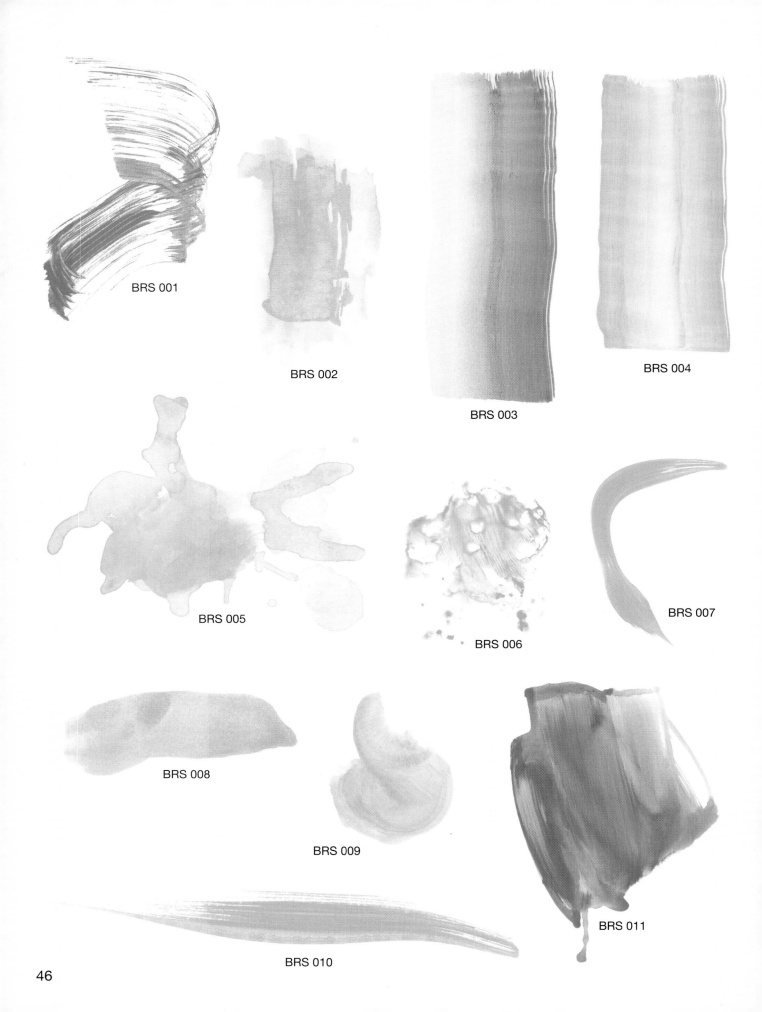

BRS 001

BRS 002

BRS 003

BRS 004

BRS 005

BRS 006

BRS 007

BRS 008

BRS 009

BRS 010

BRS 011

BRS 013

BRS 014

BRS 012

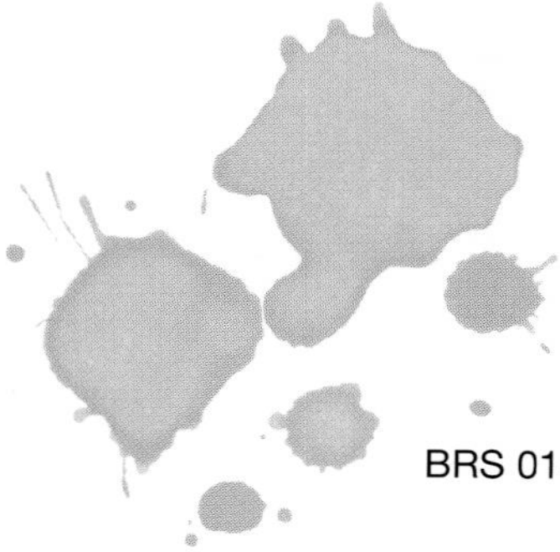

BRS 015

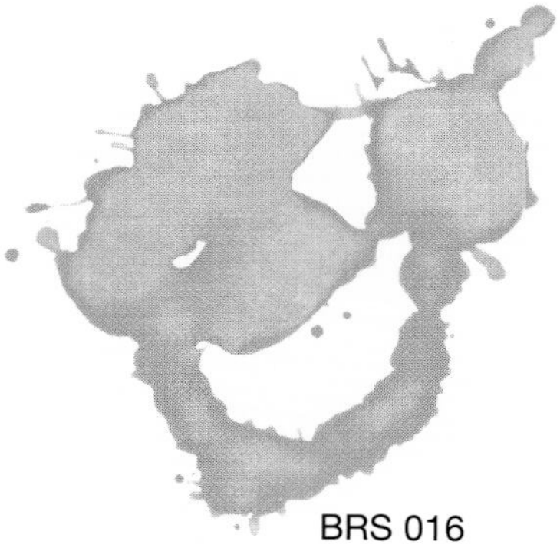

BRS 016

BRS 017

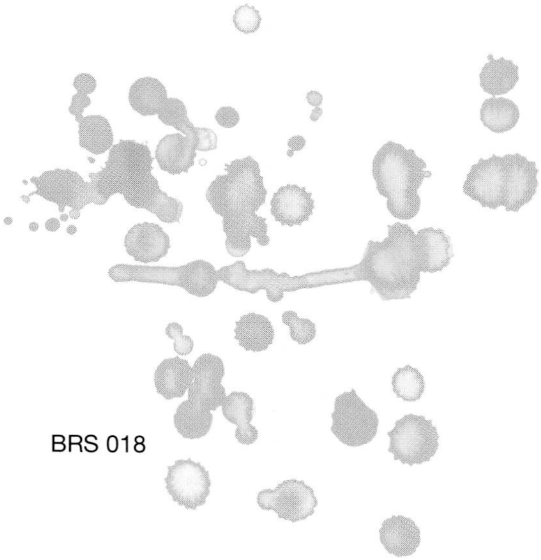

BRS 018

BRS 019

BRS 020

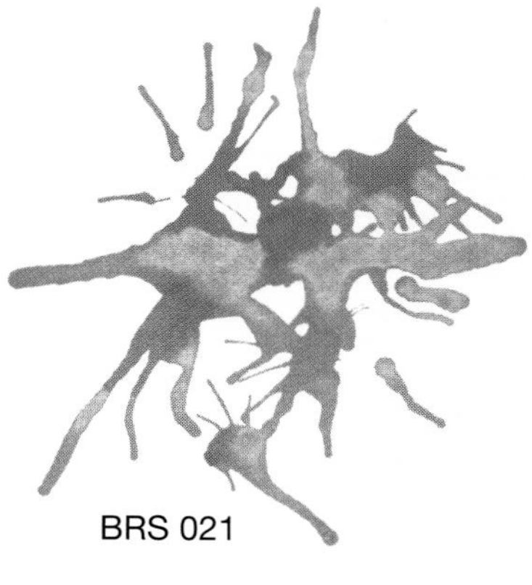

BRS 021

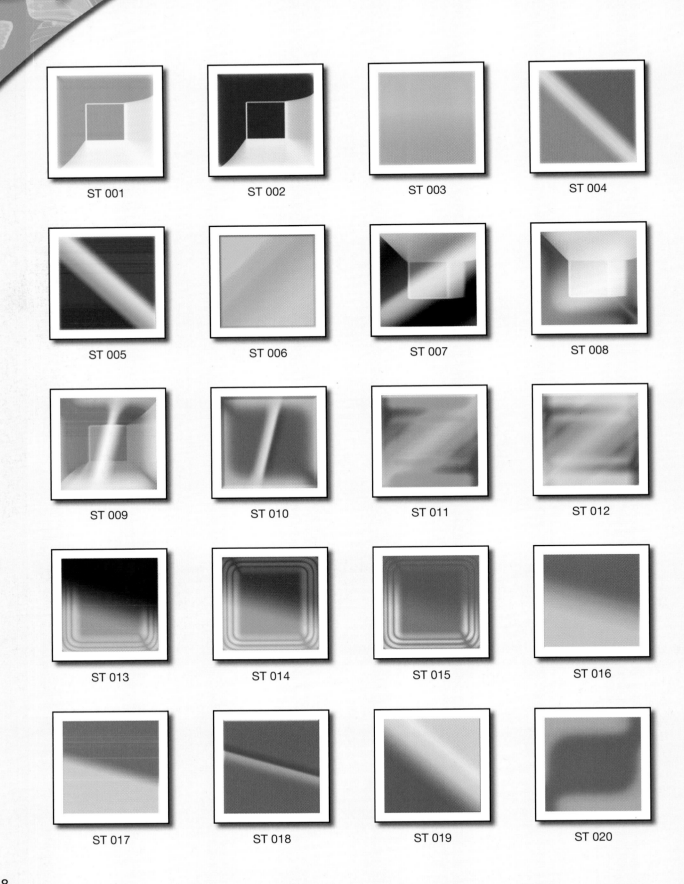

ST 001 ST 002 ST 003 ST 004
ST 005 ST 006 ST 007 ST 008
ST 009 ST 010 ST 011 ST 012
ST 013 ST 014 ST 015 ST 016
ST 017 ST 018 ST 019 ST 020